# THE WEALTH MAGICK WORKBOOK

or

*BUDDY, CAN YOU SPARE A PARADIGM?*

by

Dave Lee

6th Revised Edition

published by

*attractor*

January 2013 c.e.

For all those magicians of the IOT

who joined in when I suggested

we help each other find ways

to become wealthier

© Dave Lee 1994, 1999, 2000, 2005, 2011, 2012

All rights reserved. No part of this publication may be reproduced, stored in a retrieval system or transmitted, in any form or by any means, electronic, mechanical, photocopying, recording or otherwise, without the prior permission of the publishers.

# CONTENTS

**FOREWORD** 7

**INTRODUCTION: LUST FOR LIFE** 9

WEALTH AND MONEY 11

## PART 1: MONEY MAGICKS

### MONEY TECH 1: DISCS AND DESIRES

MONEY PSYCHOLOGY: SELF-ESTEEM 14
EXERCISES
MONEY PSYCHOLOGY: SECURITY 18
EXERCISES
MONEY SORCERY: MONEY AS A MAGICKAL OBJECT 20
EXERCISES
COIN RITUAL 23

## MONEY TECH 2 : STALKING THE MONEY SPIRIT

THE VALUE ZONE: VALUES AROUND WEALTH

| | |
|---|---|
| AND MONEY | 25 |
| MONEY SYMBOLISM | 26 |
| WORK, TRADE AND INVESTMENT | |
| – THE MERCURY SPIRIT | 28 |
| EXERCISES | |
| MONEY MANAGEMENT | 32 |
| INVESTMENT | 34 |
| EXERCISES | |
| MAGNIFICENCE AND LUCK | |
| - THE SPIRIT OF JUPITER | 37 |
| EXERCISES | |
| DARK BEAUTY – PLUTO | 39 |
| EXERCISES | |
| | |
| MONEY SHAMANISM: THE NATURE OF | |
| THE MONEY SPIRIT | 41 |
| EXERCISES | |
| A WORKING: MONEY IN THE SPIRIT VISION | 44 |
| MONEY EVOCATION | 46 |
| A VIRTUAL EVOCATION | 48 |

## PART 2 : WEALTH MAGICK AGAIN  51

| | |
|---|---|
| THE HIERARCHY OF FREEDOM | 54 |
| THE COST OF MONEY: HOW WEALTHY ARE YOU? | 56 |

| | |
|---|---|
| EXERCISES | |
| ENCHANTING FOR POSSESSIONS | 59 |
| EXERCISES | |
| THE RELEVANCE OF POSSESSIONS | 63 |
| EXERCISES | |
| ENCHANTING FOR EXPERIENCES | 65 |
| | |
| WEALTH MAGICK ILLUMINATION AND INVOCATION | 67 |
| | |
| PATHWORKING INVOCATION OF LORD GANESHA | 69 |

## **PART 3 : THE BIG PICTURE**     71

| | |
|---|---|
| THE MONEY SPIRIT AND ECONOMICS | 72 |
| WEALTH AND TIME | 75 |
| INFLUENCING THE MACRO-ECONOMY | 79 |

## **APPENDICES**

| | |
|---|---|
| 1. DISCOVERY WRITING | 82 |
| 2. THE PERCENTAGE BUDGET | 84 |
| 3. WELL FORMED OUTCOMES | 86 |
| 4. A RETIREMENT | 88 |
| 5. EVALUATION OF WEALTH AND MONEY MAGICK TECHNIQUES | 92 |

*ABOUT THE AUTHOR*     96

# FOREWORD TO THE 2013 EDITION

I wrote this book in 1994 as a *pharmakon*, a remedy for the semi-slacker, a condition I would define as a high-energy, creative person without a career structure. I'd tried all sorts of magical workings to find work, to come up with and carry out money making schemes or simply to get money to appear. Some of these spells worked, most of them didn't, or at least not as well as I'd have liked. In the course of my magical development, raising myself from the basic wealth of the semi-slacker to the next level, which requires a bit more hard cash, regularly, became the hardest magic I'd ever done.

I still have most of the root attitudes around money I had then – including a loathing for most regular employment, a contempt for most of the rewards promised for such enslavement, and a passion for personally meaningful work.

Eventually, I learned a few magical tricks; some of them are in this book. The core message is the same, so I'll state it as clearly as I can: you will only obtain great riches by getting obsessed with money, making it central to every moment of your life. If that's you, I doubt this book will be much use to you; it is designed for the person who wants enough money to do his or her will in the world, but to whom money is not an end in itself. That is wealth, and such a person will be unwilling to make the great sacrifice that the acquisition of riches entails. This book is a manual on how to fine-tune your magical life, so as to make wealth inevitable for you, so as to make the most of your freedom.

Dave Lee<br>
Sheffield, England

# INTRODUCTION: LUST FOR LIFE

## WHY MONEY MAGICK?

Most people take money seriously, but would tell you that the only way to get more is to work harder. The bad news is that this is basically true: in the long term, magick represents the fine-tuning of one's approach to money, not a guaranteed substitute for work. Further, many magicians don't take money magick very seriously, believing it to be below their notice. Why go to all the trouble of doing magick to get something as worthless as money? Leaving aside for now the question of whether wealth and money are the same thing (they're not), the answer points to two basic drives:

Insecurity, which is the negative motivation for money, and desire, which is the positive reason. The First Circuit trance is concerned with biosurvival; money is a set of tokens for that basic security. Therefore, it is important to you in proportion to how little you've got, which is to say how insecure you feel.

Money is more linked to insecurity, wealth to desire.

Desire is the drive to what has been called Blue Magick. In Pete Carroll's exposition of 8 Magicks (see *Liber Kaos*), Wealth Magick is attributed to Blue. The primary attribute of Blue Magick is desire: desire for possessions, desire for experience, desire for sex, desire for fame or recognition, desire for new talents, desire for magickal power – all of these things are the primary quality of desire acting upon your life. Blue connotes expansion, and so does desire. Blue magick is an expression of the magician's lust for life. Desire is the motive force behind growth. Without desire, nothing moves, nothing develops, nothing evolves. By desiring something, we expand the range of our world in our imagination. The art and science of bringing this expanded world into manifestation are the technologies of Blue Magick.

The techniques of Money Magick are quite different from the techniques that work best to enhance Wealth. The two approaches are reflected in the structure of this book.

# WEALTH AND MONEY

It should not have to be said that money and wealth are not the same thing. However, people both poor and rich do mix them up, so I'll say it anyway: Money does not constitute wealth. Naturally, if you are wealthy, you have sufficient money at any moment. Similarly, if you have a "large" sum of money, you can live a wealthy life if you want to. But the terms Money and Wealth are not interchangeable: the person who inherits or wins half a million could, with an enjoyable degree of effort, ensure a ready supply of money for the rest of any lifespan. Or blow it in no time at all.

Wealth does not consist of money; ultimately, it has only marginally to do with money at all. So what constitutes wealth?

Wealth is abundance where and when you want it. To elaborate, to be wealthy is to live your life the way you want to. The condition of wealth is the experience of confidence, relevance and abundant pleasure in one's material environment.

Money is a parameter, whose value is arbitrary and impersonal; Wealth is a skill, whose value is arbitrary, and personal.

Money is a Spirit, an elemental; Wealth is the attribute of a God.

OK, I've said all I'm going to say for a few chapters about the distinction between money and wealth. Now I'll get straight into what you want to read about: Magicks for Money.

# MONEY TECH 1

## DISCS AND DESIRES

# MONEY PSYCHOLOGY: SELF-ESTEEM

Undoubtedly one of the chief barriers to wealth and money is low self esteem. If, at some level of your internal monologue, there is a voice saying 'I don't deserve to be well off, I don't deserve to have more money' and so forth, then however sophisticated your magicks, they will mostly fail. Therefore, work on your self-esteem, your sense of worth.

A useful technique for dealing with this problem is the use of 'affirmations'. Much that is completely useless and misleading has been written about affirmations; many new age self-help people seem to think that they work on the principle of 'If you throw enough mud (or whatever) at a wall, some of it is bound to stick'. For instance, if you tell yourself 'I always feel secure', you will probably get an immediate internal voice saying 'Rubbish, what about that time the other day I got stuck in such and such a place with no cash...' etc. etc. Don't worry about this; the purpose of using affirmations is not to lie to yourself until you believe you believe it, but to loosen the girders of belief a bit, to work on old embedded responses and expose the internal monologue that keeps them in place. When you get a response like that, it's a sign that the process is working. Change the phrase you were using just a little, shifting its emphasis, and try again. Simply repeating the phrase, 'listening' for your own emotional/physical reaction, and then repeating it again, is a good place to start, and may be all you need.

Flex the muscles of desire and positive self image by using the following exercises.

**EXERCISES**

i)      Consider your desire for money. Consider it a lot. Not while you're doing a particular working or ritual - that would only serve to bring lust of result to the conscious level - but as a general mental process informing your life. Know you have a right to that desire, and yet tell yourself you would be a fool to attach yourself to that desire.

ii)     Think about money and observe your feelings about it. Write down these phrases and repeat them to yourself:

> *I love money*
> *I enjoy money*
> *There is no such thing as having too much money*
> *When I have a lot of extra money I enjoy it.*

- and other similar positive phrases. Pay careful attention to the feelings in your body as you repeat each sentence. When the feeling is unpleasant or 'dubious', re-phrase the sentence and try again. Keep on doing this until you feel a real glow of pleasure at the idea you have phrased.

In this way, you begin to tune your mind in to positive attitudes about money. Let your desire focus in on money, on receiving money, on having money, on spending money. Visualize money flowing through your hands, pockets, wallet, purse. Keep this exercise up, creating new affirmations and fine-tuning them through observing your responses and adjusting the phrasing.

Finish on a positive statement!

### ✷✷✷ *REALLY IMPORTANT POINT!* ✷✷✷

*In continuity with the traditions of books about money magick, I'm about to tell you one of the genuine, simple 'secrets' of success in any form of enchantment: It is to refine your intention, to specify your desire so that it achieves complete congruence with every aspect of your will. This is so simple, and yet virtually all magickal failure stems from ignorance of this principle. A unified will can do infinitely more than a divided will. Some of the exercise in this book relate directly to this principle. Keep it in front of your thoughts at all times you are doing magick. In the Appendices, a technique from Neuro-Linguistic Programming, (NLP) is give, Well Formed Outcomes, which is well worth mastering for this purpose.*

# MONEY PSYCHOLOGY: SECURITY

Obviously, money has powerful emotional dimensions. Generally, people feel pretty insecure when they're not carrying some form of money. On the other hand, when you have, in terms of the local economy you're in at the time, lots of the stuff, you tend to feel more secure and confident. In *Prometheus Rising*, Robert Anton Wilson traces this anxiety/security seesaw to the First or Biosurvival Circuit. As a brief digression, the 8 Circuits are seen as levels or zones in the nervous system which are imprinted by key events in the individual's history. The first circuit is to do with avoiding pain/approaching pleasure, and is rooted in the imprints that the baby gets from its mother's care - feeding or having to wait for food, warmth/cold, being cuddled or being isolated, etc.

These imprints orientate the character in the direction of physical insecurity or physical security. Typically, dysfunctions on this circuit are felt as whole body sensations, rather than specific emotions. Desire for anaesthesia or for food bingeing relate to this level. So does money.

**EXERCISES**

1. Try such phrases as the following out on yourself, and see how you feel:

   *I am my own source of security*

   *I always feel secure*

Phrases like these always bring up some negative response. As discussed above, this is a sign that the process is working. Remember: Nothing is true, everything is permitted !

2. Meditate on the biological function of money. Consider money as biosurvival tokens. See how this concept links up with your feelings of security or insecurity.

3. Meditate on the social & emotional functions of money. Next time you spend or receive some, reflect on the meaning to the other party of parting with money, and the meaning to you of receiving it.

The exercises above should have begun to acquaint you with, or remind you of, the emotional dimensions of money.

# MONEY SORCERY:

# MONEY AS A MAGICKAL OBJECT

Money has some curious properties. For a start, all similar banknotes are almost exactly identical, bar the serial number and degree of wear. Banknotes have weird pictures on them, rendered in such complex detail that they are relatively hard to forge. The British banknotes have little scenes from the lives of famous people on them. The US notes have the infamous Eye in the Pyramid glyph, beloved of conspiracy theorists.

Nearly everybody has money. It is almost as common an attribute as having two eyes or two legs. Money is an excellent object through which to work sorcery, which is the manipulation of symbolic objects to magickal effect. To get into the sorceries of money, try the following exercises.

**EXERCISES**

1. Learn to pay attention to money. When someone hands you money, look at the coins, the notes, the cheques... Banknotes in particular are complex talismans, beautiful and somewhat mysterious. Acquaint yourself with these magick pictures. Feel your money, sniff it, rub it between your hands, caress it. Quietly observe your own reactions.
2. Make a list of 20 things you can see in a banknote.
3. Meditate on the universality of money, the way it turns up everywhere. Think of money in your pocket, in other people's pockets, in houses, offices, factories, shops, on buses and aeroplanes.
4. Consider the uniformity of notes and coins. Make a row of identical coins or notes and look at them, gaze at them, let ideas come into your mind. Play with them like a child might.

Sorcery is a very direct and primal approach to magick. Any magickal act which manipulates material objects to symbolize directly the intention of the rite is a kind of act of sorcery. The exercises above will have prepared you for designing and performing magickal workings based around the direct use of money.

So, what are the ingredients of a successful magickal working?

Firstly, you need an altered state of consciousness, often referred to by Chaos magicians as *gnosis*. The core actions of the working are performed in this state.

Gnosis can be reached through any means which serves to dislocate the normal internal dialogue and generate a fanatical one-pointedness of concentration. Often-used methods include: sex, with or without a partner; mild doses of intoxicants; prolonged meditation to still the mind; dancing; chanting/singing; overbreathing, etc etc. When the required intensity has been reached, the sorcerer takes the magickal objects and performs upon them the transformations which symbolize the desired result.

A simple example would be the spell that follows.

# COIN RITUAL

Take a coin or banknote, and a small vessel of water, to a place out of doors where plants are growing, and where you will not be disturbed. Perform any banishing or orientation exercise you require, or simply meditate quietly until you are ready to proceed.

You are going to consecrate the piece of money as a seed. Gaze at the money, and appreciate it. Begin to talk to it, telling it that it is a seed that will grow into a great tree. Move around, offering it to the sun, to the rains, to the earth, to the other plants, so that it becomes more and more identified with a seed in your mind. Work your movements up into a dance, of growth and life.

When you have reached the highest state of ecstasy you can, when your identification of the money with a seed is at its height, plant the seed in the ground. Water it, repeat your final blessings over it, and banish with laughter.

Obviously, this kind of rite can be elaborated further. The 'seed' can be nourished with blood or a sexual elixir from your own body. One of the main points, though, is to enjoy the rite, then forget the 'seed', leave it behind and banish it from your mind thereafter.

# MONEY TECH 2:

# STALKING THE MONEY SPIRIT

# THE VALUE ZONE:

## VALUES AROUND WEALTH AND MONEY

Just as it's vitally important to understand one's unconscious reflexes to money, other important keys to your financial condition can be found by looking at your values - what things you put first and second in your life. These values are criteria for making decisions, and analyzing which way you will decide between two or more options reveals them. They are often unconscious, and this can be deeply unhelpful in understanding your relationship with money. Each of the following sections contains exercises which can help you to understand your values around money.

# MONEY SYMBOLISM

Modern money is increasingly like a spirit. It has been abstracted from useful possessions like cattle (the rune *FEHU* in the Elder Futhark), through semi-useless lumps of 'precious' (i.e. rare) metals, through coins and banknotes, through cheques and promissory notes, to pure number, stored in computers. Ever since money came into being, it has been pursued by magicians, and they have left their traces in the symbolism attached to it. Some people like to work with the Planets of classical magick. These work on different areas of money and wealth, as follows:-

**Jupiter** symbolizes Wealth itself. The King of the Gods has among his attributes confidence, serenity, and power. Jupiter has always been associated with wealth more than money, but appears in money symbolism as the Lord of Luck.

**Mercury** has long been associated with trade and business, skill and theft. Knowledge of the manipulation of money comes under Mercury (obviously including bookkeeping and accountancy). The planning and structuring of a business or money making operation would therefore come under Mercury.

The darkest glamours and most dangerous aspects of money come under **Pluto**. In the Roman myths the god of the Underworld was Pluto. Therefore, Pluto was also the Lord of mines, of hidden gold. Pluto is also associated with the underworld in the criminal sense - gangsterism and organized crime, the secret pursuits of money.

**Venus** rules those things we take pleasure in, and so is used in workings for possessions.

Other planetary dynamics may be used by the money magician, especially if he is constructing a business along magickal lines. In this case, he might require **Saturn** for budgeting, **Uranus** for inspiration, **Sun** for projection of personal qualities, and so on.

In order to get a glimpse of the faces of the Money Spirit, we'll look at it under the headings of the main planetary attributions above.

# WORK, TRADE AND INVESTMENT: THE MERCURY SPIRIT

## WORK & TRADE

So far I might have given the (mistaken) impression that I believe there is little or no connection between money magicks and working for a living. The Mercury aspect of money covers our attitudes to working for it, and other forms of conscious planning and effort. Attitudes to work are vitally important to a good relationship with the money spirit.

The distinction between wealth and money is pointed up vividly by your attitude to work: What is the point of working at a job you hate in order to get the money which you will spend in obliterating the misery and frustration of your working day?

Many of the problems associated with work are due to the form of the work : working for someone else, in a job. In my experience and in that of many others, self employment is the ideal form of employment for the magician, and is nothing like as unstable as many people believe. There is no stability in the labour market in any case - people of all ages, levels of experience and in all kinds of jobs lose their jobs these days. Job security is an hallucination in nearly all cases. The adventurous magician would be much better off designing his own form of income generation.

The outlook of the self-employed trader is strongly supported by the following fact: All income is derived from sales. This doesn't just apply to the salesperson; consider where all businesses get their money from to pay their employees: from selling products or services. Therefore, one skill that all self-employed persons need is the ability to sell their product or service.

When we go on to consider that all products and services were once ideas in someone's mind, we are approaching recognizably magickal territory. Ideas are the result of creative processes, so can be said to originate in the Chaos of the mind's quantum core.

To summarize:
*All income comes from sales of products or services;*
*All products and services start off as ideas;*
*All ideas originate in the creative mind.*

This formula is capable of being restated in numerous ways. It can be compressed to:

*ALL WEALTH AND ALL MAGICK IS SUPPORTED BY FREEDOM !*

EXERCISES

1. Imagine your ideal work: What would you be doing on your typical day ? What kind of people would you work with and meet in the course of the day ? Think of what you put your love of life into, and imagine working at something that has that enthusiasm behind it.

2. Turn to Appendix 1, *Discovery Writing*. Do the exercises there to acquaint yourself with this technique. Then do the discovery list: 20 ENJOYABLE WAYS FOR ME TO MAKE A LIVING. Pick 3 that you might be able to make money out of. For each of these 3, write a list of how you might do this.

3. Plan how you would make a living out of something you enjoy doing, and what magickal workings you would use to support it over the first year.

**Values:** Considering your actual behaviour, which do you value more?

1. A direct action approach to increasing your income, or a wait-and-hope approach?

2. Work satisfaction, or the satisfaction of the money you get by working? (Or are you working because you desperately need the money it brings you?)

3. Working for your financial success or ensuring the success of your personal relationships?

4. Time at work or leisure time?

# MONEY MANAGEMENT

Another Mercurial facet of money is financial planning. Most people suffer from debt problems to a greater or lesser extent. This is no accident; the banking system makes most of its money out of lending at interest, and so it is in the interest of the banks that people feel anxious about money, and desire a quick fix of cash to gratify desires, which are largely generated by consumerist society. The long term solution to debt problems does not lie in the magickal dimensions. A successful spell may extricate you from a particular financial crisis, but without addressing the bad money habits that cause you to go into debt you will simply fall back into crisis again.

If you are prone to such problems, a solid, down-to-earth approach to reorganization of your finances is required. Plenty of books are available on this area, but for those who are interested I have included the basic method of percentage budgeting in *Appendix 2*.

One further word about planning: Plan for Success ! Organize your life so that you are always creating new inlets for money. When you work for large sums of money, make sure you have opened plenty of channels of manifestation. Otherwise, you may get it by your Uncle Ernest dropping dead and leaving you your stake in his will, or your lover being crippled in an accident and getting compensation.

**Values:** Considering your behaviour, which do you value more:

1. Saving or spending money?

2. Leaving bills as long as possible or paying them straight away?

3. Borrowing money to get what you want now, or living within your means?

4. Budgeting and planning, or a more laid-back approach to managing your money?

5. Recording your outgoings, or being more casual about how you spent your money?

# INVESTMENT

It appears that the money spirit loves to reproduce itself, multiplying through investment. This is partly a consequence of investment in wealth-creation, i.e. lending money at interest to those who sell products or services, and getting a cut of their profits back on top of your stake. It is also partly a consequence of an arbitrary feature of money built into it by those who run the banking system, which allows money to be issued which represents nothing except the policies of the bankers. At present, it is difficult if not impossible to separate these aspects of the money spirit's reproductive function. I'll come back to this point later.

The function of investment is to give yourself an income without working for it. This is the financial freedom that most people aspire to, but not all achieve. Without some form of consistent investment strategy, you are not taking control of your financial future. Again, many people, including magicians, have negative feelings about investment and saving. The solution here is to examine what it is you want out of investment, then discipline yourself to save.

EXERCISES

1. Meditate on the sentence:- MONEY MAKES MONEY BETTER THAN WORK MAKES MONEY !

It is not suggested for a moment that you regard this statement as true for longer than it takes you to understand the mind-set of the investor. Many people are uneasy about investment, either because they don't understand it (because they've never done it, or have done it and haven't thought about it), or out of reservations about the ecological or humanitarian effects of it, or even because they believe the financial system that supports it will have collapsed before they are able to draw their pension. For better or worse, we are all embedded in capitalist economics, and it is important to understand the cornerstone of capitalism - investment - and evaluate its usefulness to yourself.

**Values** around investment:
1. Ask yourself what your reservations (if any) about investment are.
2. Consider whether there are better options than investing in companies, such as investing in yourself or friends' enterprises.
3. Consider whether your reservations can be overcome by fine-tuning, or whether you find yourself against investing, full ctop.
4. Ask yourself what level of security would be required for you to invest in something.
5. Considering your actual behaviour, do you prefer to take risks to make money, or to earn money with low-risk ways of making an income?

# MAGNIFICENCE AND LUCK: THE SPIRIT OF JUPITER

The character of Jupiter is kingly, benign, expansive, and confident. The Jupiter current itself therefore belongs more in the magicks of Wealth than that of Money, and so I'll deal with it later. In money magicks, Jupiter appears as the Lord of Luck.

Luck is one of those elusive qualities which a magician should be interested in; wherever chance operates in life, there is room for magickal influence.

For those who are thinking of setting up a magickally-run business which has a very public face: Jupiter is traditionally associated with the world of publishing.

**EXERCISES**

Learn to attune yourself to your feelings, the signals in your body, around the issues of luck, using the following approach:

1. Ask yourself whether a particular action or plan is a good idea, and 'listen' for the sensations.
2. Ask yourself how lucky you are feeling, and feel what happens. Learn what these body-sensations mean in terms of your luck.
3. Experiment with trusting your 'lucky' feelings.

One form of money magick which gets written about a lot, usually in the more primitive and superstitious books on the subject, is gambling magick. The people whom such books are directed at may view gambling as the only possible source of additional money. This is almost total nonsense: it makes sense to do the Pools or enter a big lottery only if you don't rely on it to make you rich. It's not only fantastically unlikely that you'll win such a lottery and get rich, but your very dependence on such a hope will vitiate your attempts to get money by more certain means.

# *DARK BEAUTY*
# PLUTO

Under the surface of money, under its official faces, lies the hidden world of money. This is where money shades into political power (plutocracy and corruption), organized crime, insider trading and large-scale corporate fraud. The images associated with this aspect of money are highly glamorous, in the way that power is sexy.

This is not a particularly useful area of symbolism for basic money magick, but it does have a strong influence on how money is perceived as power and sexuality. It is worth meditating on in order to integrate the feelings you experience when exposed to that glamour. All images of power can be useful to a magician.

## EXERCISES

1. Meditate on the dark glamours of money. Run images of secret and powerful aspects of money through your mind. Observe your feelings about these images, and employ a light, detached attitude to them. The purpose of this exercise is to contact a particular aspect of Money, enjoy it and liberate yourself from attachment to it, so that you can appreciate it and use it magickally.

2. Consider your own behaviour and let it reveal whether you :
a) admire the values of the poor or the values of the rich more?
b) value paying taxes honestly or cheating on them?

# MONEY SHAMANISM

## THE NATURE OF THE MONEY SPIRIT

Let us return to viewing Money as a Spirit, something alive in our common inner worlds, something with its own magickal character. What are the attributes of this Money Spirit? It is often seen as mindless or nearly mindless; this gives rise to the popular image of Mammon, a force of blind and brutal greed. However, this image is judgmental, and too imprecise for our purposes. I think of the Money Spirit as being like the great Elemental Kings of the Enochian psychocosm, with their endless Names of howling and soughing vowels. A vast, impersonal elemental force, money flows and flashes down the circuits of communication systems, its true

Name hidden in its countless billions upon billions of alphanumeric digits.

The Nature of Money is reproduction, movement. It withers if kept still; it loves to move. It is important that money changes hands, important that it reproduces by trade and investment. It has enormous power over people's lives, over the decisions they make, over the choices of how they spend their time. It is responsible for great motivation, great misery and great stupidity.

Having acquainted yourself with some features of the Money Spirit, you can investigate it further in your own inner worlds. The exploration of the spirits of things through trance work comes under Shamanism.

There are no doubt those who would object to my characterization of money as a spirit in the shamanic sense. In answer, I would point to the attitudes of an old Amazon Basin shaman I saw interviewed on a TV programme a few years ago. This old man had been displaced, along with other members of his tribe, when they refused to accept the violently-imposed Christianity of the loggers and their missionaries. They had set up a community together with other refugees from the clearance areas, and continued to practice their ancient ways.

Just before the occasion of the interview, the shaman's son had taken him into a town for the first time. They had ridden on a bus and gone to see a film at the cinema. The old man was tremendously excited by all this; he had lived all his life in the forest, and had learned the spirit songs of animals, plants, rivers, elemental forces. Suddenly he had been precipitated into an environment where he knew very few of the spirit songs. To him, a car or a cinema was as worthy a subject of a spirit quest as any creature or object he had been brought up with. He told the interviewer how he was performing his spirit vision quests to learn to sing the song of the car, and the song of the cinema ! Since these things were now in his mind, part of his mental environment, he saw no reason why they should not have songs, songs that would be his tools for improving his power relationships with them. Such an approach is far away from the guilt ridden anti-technology attitudes of new age "shamans", and is of the essence of the ancient current.

## EXERCISES

1. Consider the things that the Money Spirit likes and dislikes. Treat it as a consciousness, with its own powers, impulses and drives.

2. Start talking to the money spirit. Make friends with it.

Try out the phrase: I LOVE MONEY AND MONEY LOVES ME

3. Get deeper into the feel of money, as a detached aesthetic process without ethical, social or political dimensions. Experiment with sigillizing from a banknote, using semi automatic drawing, as follows:

a) Gaze at the note, then close your eyes.

b) Open them while gazing at a blank piece of paper, and begin to doodle, basing your doodle on the remembered image of the banknote.

c) Repeat the process by gazing at the doodle, closing your eyes and opening them again to a fresh sheet of paper, and then drawing again.

d) Repeat the process until the sigil 'feels right'; or, to put it another way, until the process feels 'complete'.

e) This finished sigil is a gateway into the Spirit of the Banknote. (If you are not familiar with sigilization through semi-automatism, consult *The Book of Pleasure* by Austin Osman Spare, or *Visual Magick* by Jan Fries. Both books include exercises that can be used as warm-ups for this kind of sigil making. The Jan Fries book is much clearer for the beginner).

4. Devise a Shamanic Vision Quest to bring you more into contact with the Money Spirit. An example is as follows:

# *A WORKING:*
## MONEY IN THE SPIRIT VISION

Prepare your Temple, or find an outdoor working space where you will be undisturbed. Prepare yourself with exercises such as those above.

Prepare a simple chant addressed to the Money Spirit, such as: I LOVE MONEY AND MONEY LOVES ME, MONEY I WISH TO JOURNEY TO YOUR WORLD AND MEET YOU, etc etc..

Make a Money Sigil as outlined above.

Ready yourself for trance. Close your eyes. Prolonged pranayama or brief hyperventilation are useful. Use a rattle or a drum, or simply two sticks, to produce a hypnotic repetitious rhythm.

Begin your chant, repeating it continuously, letting it change and develop as inspiration dictates. Begin to visualize yourself in darkness, with swirling forms just beyond your sight. Feel that you are passing underground, into the realm of spirits.

When the trance feels deep enough, visualize the money sigil like a doorway, continue your chant, and pass through it. You are in the realm of the Money Spirit.

Now describe what you see, out loud. This will help to focus your attention, prevent you drifting off, and facilitate recall of the details at the end of the rite.

As your inner senses lock into the feeling of the Money Spirit, begin to talk to it, addressing it out loud. Make friends with it. Listen to its replies and repeat them out loud. Make requests of it, if you wish.

When you are satisfied with the working, or cannot go any further, thank the Money Spirit, and depart from its world, talking yourself back into the outer world.

This type of working can be further developed through the use of a power animal, if you have one.

# MONEY EVOCATION

Evocation is the creation of servitors (or the summoning of spirits) for the performance of particular tasks. A servitor is a kind of entity that is budded off from the magician's consciousness whilst in gnosis, usually with a set of instructions embedded in its structure.

Some magicians like to think of servitors as conscious entities of a different order of life, rather like animal spirits. Cybernetic paradigms are also popular, where the magician regards the entity as a kind of 'astral machine' with a programming facility which contains a set of instructions. Yet another view of servitors is based on a genetic model, in which the servitor is a set of instructions (like a DNA code) that replicates itself automatically under the right conditions (like a virus). Whichever model we use, the usefulness of a servitor resides mainly in two features: i) it remains functioning in the astral/aetheric dimensions for a prolonged period of time, working automatically when the conditions are correct, and ii) it can be called on to perform particular tasks readily, without going through an entire ritual again. Experienced users of servitors will often have a number of them 'waiting in the wings' for different purposes. when the need arises, the magician simply visualizes the servitor (or calls it in some other way) and instructs it to act as desired.

In money evocation we are creating an individual, independent entity with a designated relationship with the spirit of money. Techniques of servitor creation are many and varied. At the level of sorcery, a material base might be created, which is then empowered as a fetish. A shamanic approach might be to journey in the spirit vision to capture an elemental ally and instruct it. In ritual magick, a material base may be created and subjected to a full consecration according to whatever system of magick is chosen. The following example uses a pathworking, in which the servitor is created purely by pre-programmed visualization in light trance. If one's powers of visualization are good enough, a material base is not needed for this kind of servitor.

# A VIRTUAL EVOCATION

For a virtual experience of the money spirit, and the construction of a servitor from it, try the following pathworking.

Preparation: you will need to decide what you are going to program the servitor with. It may also be helpful to decide on a name for it beforehand, to use in conjunction with its visual image when summoning it. A name can be constructed from letters picked out of a desire sentence, or chosen by some form of divination, or by any method that appeals to you. Alternatively, you can learn the name of the servitor in the course of the pathworking.

Go into light trance breathing, and begin to visualize:

What is the first image of money that comes to mind? Hold it as a visual image steady in your gaze. It is a doorway, which swings open in a storm of glittering dust.

You step out onto a grey space, the air like packed dust pressing against your senses. Then you detect a humming, a throb which appears to be in the bass section but moves through the whole spectrum to ultrasound.

Suddenly, the grey shatters and you are moving at speed through a flat, synthetic landscape with intermittent organic forms. You are moving so fast you cannot identify these. The cyberscape is a blur of colour, with a sparking blue haze.

You slow down, and float high above the cyberscape, the details now visible. Swarming wires in fluorescent ropes and cables, the fantastic detail of logic circuitry blown up to this vast scale, massive transfers of detailed information. Streaming through sparkling conduits of copper wire is a blue haze of Money.

You pick out structures like traffic interchanges. As your eyes zoom in on them, you realize that they are markets, money flowing through them in a stream.... billions of hands in millions of market places...

Then there are structures like giant servitors, making up banks, stock markets, subsidy systems. These are so complex that they have a dull sort of semi-autonomy, bloated and soaked through with the vast power of money. You pause and reflect that this lumbering quality invariably works to the benefit of the clever magician.

Rise up through the matrix, up, up through the swarming information streams. You rise until you are floating high above the details of the cyberscape. You are in a part of the matrix that is flooded with sparkling light which tingles through you with exquisite pleasure. You look up, through the seething brilliance, to where a gigantic Chaosphere hangs.

Know this: From the source of pure chaos comes the brilliance of mind, wherein is the true home of the Spirit of Money. As you gaze into the space before you, something takes shape. A macroform condenses out of the ubiquitous light, egg shaped at first, and then taking on the outlines of your entity. It trembles in the light, held in place by the tension of your gaze.

Now reach into the centre, touching the substance of the servitor, and instruct it as you will.

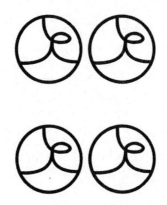

# PART 2

# WEALTH MAGICK AGAIN

In the introduction, I made a distinction between Wealth Magick and Money Magick. To expand on that distinction, there is a significant difference between wealth magick and many other magicks. You are unlikely to succeed if you just do a sigil for wealth. A servitor, permanently functioning in the aetheric dimensions, is nearer the mark.

The basic skills of Enchantment and Evocation may not, on their own, be enough. We need to work in the disciplines of Invocation and Illumination, to converse with Gods and to reprogram our expectations, to find, if you like, a metaprogrammer state from which to renegotiate the conditions of the selves. To put it simply, money is to wealth like sex drive is to skill at sexual relationships.

*Money is a parameter, whose value is arbitrary and impersonal:*
*Wealth is a skill, whose value is arbitrary, and personal.*
*Money is a Spirit, an elemental; Wealth is the attribute of a God.*

In fact, it is the relevance of possessions and experiences to your desires that matters. Considering that these terms are subjective, the work consists of defining what kind of magician you want to become. Success in this process liberates the power to attain the sphere of material control that you desire. As a wealth magician, you practice the art and science of living your life as you wish.

The point is, we are looking at a long term change here. In the words of the song, money won't change you. But wealth will; wealth is an attitude to life which is always with you, and the nature of Wealth Magick is the acquisition of Wealth Consciousness. Wealth Consciousness is the organic belief in the inevitability of wealth for you.

Let us return to the planetary model, and see what use we can make of the symbols.

The restless Mercurial qualities of the money spirit, its affinity with communication hierarchies and networks has led to the suggestion that Air would be a better elemental attribution than the Discs of Earth. There is some usefulness in this concept - if we can get away from the idea of money as coins in our pockets, we are one step closer to the concept of Wealth.

Jupiter symbolizes Wealth itself. The King of the Gods has among his attributes confidence, serenity, and power. I'll go into the attributes of the Gods of Wealth in the section on Wealth Invocation. The next section makes the all important connection between Wealth and Freedom.

# THE HIERARCHY OF FREEDOM

The distinction between wealth and money can be spread over a spectrum, illustrating the different emphases that magick will have at each level:

The wealthy individual is free, enjoying the material resources he desires, playing with the kingly grace of a creature at the top a food chain, a big cat or bird of prey. The world of a truly wealthy person is held together by a resource of joyous power that stems from the experience of radical freedom at the innermost core, the quantum chaos of consciousness. Without the will to play confidently in the world, everything stays at the crudest and most temporary level of money magick.

The next level down, the magician realizes that the only things worth enchanting for are experiences, conditions of life which fulfill his dreams. The identification of one's driving dream, and the knowledge of the resources needed to realise it, form a large part of the work at this level.

The spectrum now slides away from freedom, towards enslavement, towards obsessional insecurity about money. Many people who are competent at making money are terribly insecure about their survival and status, so that their money does not bring them wealth in the above sense - only more obsession with making more money, which is hardly freedom. Such people are workaholics or wage slaves. Each day, each paycheque, each repetition of the same meaningless task - this is the key to the demonic aspect of the money spirit, that its mastery over you will lead to immersion in boring repetition and routine.

The worst condition is the *poverty well*. Like a gravity well, this warps perspective. It pulls wealth and money together so that they can't be disentangled. In the poverty well, the only parameter is cash. The poor person is enslaved to money, and will often do anything to get it. In this state, money is all-important, a continual emergency, much of the content of one's internal dialogue.

The following section enables you to quantify your freedom and wealth.

# THE COST OF MONEY: HOW WEALTHY ARE YOU?

Meditate on your desire for money. Consider times when you were:

i) Broke and happy

ii) Broke and miserable

iii) Well off & happy

iv) Well off & miserable

Since wealth consists of living your life as you please, with abundant pleasure in the resources you have, we are going to examine how the amount of leisure you have conflicts with the amount of money you earn.

The following 2 exercises will enable you to quantify the relationship between your wealth, money and work. If you haven't familiarized yourself with the Discovery Writing technique, turn to Appendix 1 and do the exercises there.

**EXERCISE 1: WEALTH AND MONEY**

a) Write the discovery list: TWENTY THINGS I ENJOY DOING REGULARLY (take 2 minutes).

b) Now choose your favourite 10 of these (take as much time as you need - this is not a discovery list)

c) Now take your 10 favourite activities and write down whether or not you would spend more money on each one if you could.

This exercise has allowed you to quantify your wealth at the present time.

## EXERCISE 2 : TIME AND WEALTH

Now take each of your 10 favourite activities again, and for each one, write down whether you would like to devote more time to it.

This exercise allows you to quantify your enslavement to money at the present time. In other words, it measures your negative wealth. Enslavement to money is the opposite of wealth.

To explain this point, let us take an example.

Suppose someone's 10 favourite daily activities, and his scores for them in exercises 1 & 2 are:

|   | EX.1 | EX.2 |
|---|---|---|
| 1 Having sex | NO | YES |
| 2 Drinking good wine | YES | NO |
| 3 Reading comics | NO | YES |
| 4 Watching TV | NO | YES |
| 5 Traveling abroad | YES | YES |
| 6 Solving crossword puzzles | NO | YES |
| 7 Working out at the gym | NO | YES |
| 8 Listening to music | NO | NO |

9 Dining out                    YES     YES
10 Playing drums                NO      YES

So, he scored 7 out of 10 in terms of the MONEY he has to spend on his activities. You could say he is 70 per cent wealthy at the time of doing this exercise!

However, he scored only 2 out of 10 in terms of the free time he has to enjoy his pastimes.

He might therefore draw the conclusion that he is spending too much time doing things he doesn't enjoy, and not earning quite enough money!

# ENCHANTING FOR POSSESSIONS

Our Wealth Magick symbol, Jupiter, connotes expansion. In terms of living the life you want, what is it that you wish to expand? One obvious answer is: Possessions. You might want your own house, a car, a stereo, a new pair of shoes. On a scale of money values, it seems obvious that the shoes are the most easily available item. However, to someone with virtually no income, a decent pair of shoes is a big expenditure. It's nothing to most people in regular paid work. A car is not such a big deal for a lot of people.

The point here is that your ability to acquire possessions depends quite strongly on what possessions you are accustomed to owning.

This aspect of Wealth Magick is summed up in the symbol of the Zone of Availability. It is illustrated by a story, of a man who was so poor that he lived in one room without even a kettle. After many days gazing around his room, he began to visualize a kettle on the work-surface. The next day, he goes out and finds a nearly new kettle, perhaps in a skip. He goes on to visualize his world bit by bit, building it up until he becomes a very wealthy man.

The moral of the tale is that he could not have done all this in one step - that when he was poor, his Zone of Availability was down to a single item of kitchenware. When he had acquired that, he was able to visualize other, more expensive possessions, so that only by successive acquisitions did his ability to visualize his wealth grow. Get yourself used to being wealthy, thinking wealthy. Build on each success, always expanding.

**EXERCISES**

**1) ZONE OF AVAILABILITY VISUALIZATION**

Close your eyes, and go into light trance breathing.

You are seated comfortably, relaxed and alert. Around you is a milky, misty haze with no detail. You are in the centre of a sphere, about 3 metres in diameter, made of a soft translucent substance.

You consider your possessions, and as you think of them, they appear inside your sphere. You go on enumerating them in your mind, until you cannot think of any more possessions. You look at the boundary of your sphere and notice that it is further away. The sphere has expanded to accommodate all of your possessions. Let your glance pass over your possessions. Consider what they mean to you, what value they have to you, what pleasure you gain from them.

Now consider them all together, and consider what reflections they are of you.

Now think about all the things that you want. They appear through the milky haze outside your sphere, their outlines becoming clearer as they get near to the boundary of the sphere. Consider each of them in turn. For each one, ask: How much do you want it? How far away do you imagine you are from possessing it?

Now let the desired objects arrange themselves in front of you. You notice that some of the desired objects are now inside your sphere. This is your current Zone of Availability. One of its properties is that it always expands. What it expands into is up to you.

Now come back, and give yourself a minute to consider what you experienced there.

## 2) INCREASING YOUR PHYSICAL ZONE OF AVAILABILITY

The ability to convince yourself that you can possess more than you have now is based on your habits. The following exercise is aimed at breaking your habits of relative poverty, and so expanding your zone of availability.

The type of exercise that you might perform at this level is to try something that is difficult for you, something you have never done before.

For instance, go to a car dealer and test drive an expensive car. Or go into a restaurant that's out of your present range of affordability and talk to the staff on some pretext or other. The experience of moving out of your usual socio-economic bracket can be disturbing, and highly instructive. Regard the experience as a rehearsal for greater social mobility and ease.

# THE RELEVANCE OF POSSESSIONS

In my definition of wealth, I mentioned relevance of material conditions. There is no point in having possessions you don't need or don't enjoy. Following the driven consumerism of this culture, many people mistake a cluttered material world for a wealthy one. Also, many magicians fail to achieve what they believe to be wealth, simply because they haven't worked out what they want the material conditions of their lives to be like.

Just because someone tells you that a BMW is the most desirable car, doesn't mean that it is of the least value to you. Just because you know that a holiday in Bali represents luxury to some people doesn't mean that it would be any more than an inconvenience involving insect bites and sunburn to you. If you go ahead and enchant for an item you don't want, it is highly likely that your own unconscious resistance to acquiring it will prevent success. Decide what you want first, then enchant for it.

**EXERCISE**

**ZONE OF RELEVANCE VISUALIZATION**

This exercise helps loosen up your concepts of desire and relevance, and see how things and their purposes fit together in your world.

Return to your Zone of Availability visualization, visualizing all your possessions.

Now consider the purposes of all the things in your world. Let your sphere contain all the things and qualities you need to set up your current daily life. This is like the Zone of Availability, but it is concerned with the purposes of your possessions.

Now add one possession you desire but do not own. How does it fit in? What use is it to you? Does owning it have any drawbacks?

Come out of this meditation and place the significant memories of the experience in long term recall.

# ENCHANTING FOR EXPERIENCES

In an earlier section I asked: What is it that you wish to expand in your life ? The answer dealt with there was: possessions. There is another useful answer: Experiences.

'Experiences' is a wider category than 'Possessions'. A possession can be considered as a source of experiences; in fact, the only reason you would want to possess any object is for some experience of utility, pleasure or whatever else it gives you. Therefore, the most general type of Wealth Magick enchantment is enchantment for experiences. Bear this in mind whenever you plan to enchant for something.

**EXERCISE**

Ask yourself: what experience do I want?

Visualize yourself doing something you've never done before, and want to do. Consider this desire in detail: how would you set it up? What possessions, money and conditions does this experience require ? and so on. Be exhaustive, considering every aspect of the experience you can think of. Don't forget to ask yourself: Is it worth the effort?

Repeat the procedure until you find an experience you definitely want to enchant for. Having decided on one, now go ahead and devise an enchantment for that experience. Don't bother enchanting for all
the bits and conditions that make it up - if you have satisfied yourself that you really want the experience, the items you require for it should be susceptible to your magick.

Try it and see !

# WEALTH MAGICK ILLUMINATION AND INVOCATION

When working for wealth, the object of Illumination is Wealth Consciousness, the organic belief in the existence and inevitability of wealth for you. Invocation can be the royal road of Illumination in wealth magick. Consider the Gods and Goddesses of Wealth and Fortune - Jupiter, Ganesha, Zeus, Hera, Mamiwater: they are mature, serene, jovial, powerful, charismatic, confident, optimistic, positive. Work with the Gods and Goddesses of Wealth and Fortune in invocation, so that you summon their aid, and become more like them yourself. Salute the expansive greatness, the massive confidence of these beings. Surround yourself with symbols of your God or Goddess, with symbols of wealth and generosity. Exalt your feelings in love and admiration to these beings, until you begin to identify with their awesome power.

Choose a God or Goddess to work with, one that resonates strongly with you. Study It mythologically, make or get a picture or a statue of It, prepare the decorations and offerings It is said to love. Devise a form of invocation suitable for the particular deity in style and content, and perform it, as often as you need to bring you to the core of the Blue Magick experience. This Working, if pursued passionately, will amount to what Crowley called an invocation of the Holy Guardian Angel, a higher state of gnosis, in which one's desires are one's True Will. If you don't feel comfortable with the True Will /HGA paradigm, you can still work with invocation for the reasons already given. Also, it is worth considering the Exercises under the section *The Cost of Money: How Wealthy Are You?*, and the exercises under *Work and Trade* which are about designing your own source of income from what you enjoy doing. All these concepts link together.

For the experienced magician, such props can be dispensed with, and the invocation performed entirely in the imagination. This is a matter of experience and also of personal taste.

One of my favourite Blue Magick deities is the Hindu god Ganesha, elephant-headed son of Shiva and Parvati. Ganesha is very much a Tantric deity, inasmuch as he represents ecstasy, and the way of ecstasy.

His association with freedom is underlined by his function as the remover of obstacles.

# PATHWORKING INVOCATION OF LORD GANESHA

Settle down and enter a light trance state. You are weightless, your astral body floating in a featureless sea of grey. The greyness closes in, compressing you, until your awareness is circumscribed by a thin tube.

You are compressed to a cylinder, then you become almost a line, a fine row of dots…

Now you are in motion. You flicker and surge, dividing rejoining, speeding in grey channels.

Suddenly you expand, and emerge as an astral replica of yourself. You are standing at the edge of a vast forest. You see a path and enter.

The light changes. Shafts of sunlight break the clouds, dappling the forest path. You hear sounds in the forest chatter, one sound emerging louder than the others, the bellow of some great creature:

The trumpeting of a bull elephant.

You emerge into a clearing, wherein dances a figure of awesome power. A gigantic elephant headed man, with a great split running down his belly is dancing wildly, his torso held together by a writhing snake. He bellows and trumpets.

The scene flickers, and Ganesha stands directly before you, dwarfing your body. You soak up his radiance, of a raging animal joy with a sweetness at its centre, a boundless confidence in life and what it has to offer.

Now the scene flickers again, and a small rodent darts across your vision. Where the dancing Ganesha stood is now a racing blur of colour and detail. Then all is still.

You retrace your steps along the path to the edge of the forest, and return to your body.

# PART 3

# THE

# BIG

# PICTURE

Like most books on magick, other than the ones designed to be pure entertainment or propaganda, this book is written for two basic kinds of reader: those who just like to read, and those who like to do something about it. In the realm of money magicks, the former will be interested in knowledge for its own sake. The latter will want to understand things which may turn out to be useful.

# THE MONEY SPIRIT AND ECONOMICS

When one starts to think about money, it comes apart at the seams. It is impossible to write a book about money and wealth without addressing the fact that money is a consensus hallucination - if everyone decided tomorrow that it was valueless, then it would lose all its value. To get some kind of handle on what money is, I'm going to characterize some of the functions of money as Attributes of the money spirit. These are:

Attribute 1: *Money as a rational and convenient substitute for barter, for facilitating free exchange of goods and services.* (This is a measured exchange, as distinct from GIFT, which exists in the realm of Pure Freedom - more on this later). Goods and services are the basis of wealth, and they are exchanged directly for money, in order to further exchange the money for more goods and services. Let us call this function of money Attribute 1, or A1 for short. This is the kind of proto-money that is traded in LETS type schemes, pure exchange value. Loans to invest in a business could theoretically also be of this kind of money, but that probably only occurs between friends. The money we have in our pockets fulfills this function whenever we simply use it to buy things.

Attribute 2: *Money as a means of creating extra money for those who accumulate enough of it, by lending to wealth creators.* Wealth creators are people who supply goods and services, which are the basis of wealth, as distinct from money. The lendees then pay the lender a share of the profits they make from trading goods and services. The money in our pockets takes on this attribute when we invest it. This function of money is a basic attribute of small -scale capitalism.

Attribute 3: *Money as a means to create more money for those with enough of it, without any relation to wealth creation.* This is a point on which the whole economic system lies systematically to us, in order to blur the distinction between money and wealth - which is ultimately the distinction between what is worthwhile and what is worthless. Trading in actual 'money markets' is an example of a money-creating activity that - in many, or most instances - generates no wealth at all. This
function of money shades into its darkest aspect: the method of issuance of money. Banks are private institutions with no loyalties other than to their owners. When they issue money, they are lending it to governments, and demanding a return on it. This is what creates most of inflation: the result is that all of us owe interest on everything to the owners of the issuing banks. This is a 'fix' perpetrated by bankers to maintain and expand their control of the world, through the manipulation of boom and crash, war and peace. Industrial capitalism would probably have transcended itself

decades ago if it wasn't for the parasitic nature of banks. The money spirit in its present form is a prisoner of the banking system, but this is not the only form the money-spirit can exist in.

To pursue this dark vision of money further, I shall take a harder look at the relationship between wealth, as I've defined it, and money.

# WEALTH AND TIME

In the warped world of Thatcherite economics, where the sacred temple of the Market Place is exalted above all human activities, making and spending money become what life is about, and nothing else really matters, no other basis for a society is possible. I would call this vision of reality the Dwarf-World. In Dwarf-World, human lives are dwarfed and reduced by such a limited concept of existence. The drive to pointless consumption and therefore pointless production means that Dwarf-World is poisoned with pollution, and inhabited by soul-dead wage-slaves. This negative view of money has to be dealt with to complete the picture.

The first issue is the direct relationship of wealth, that which enhances our lives, to the way we experience Time. Industrial society has taught us to chop up time into saleable units. Life is cut up into chunks, to be sold off on the labour market. This is the first 'fall'. The totality is lost:-

> "The distribution of time plays a fundamental role in this transformation. Man exists only part time, during his working days, as an instrument of alienated performance....free time

would be potentially available for pleasure. But the pleasure principle which governs the id is 'timeless' also in the sense that it militates against the temporal dismemberment of pleasure, against its distribution in small separated doses. A society governed by the performance principle must of necessity impose such distribution because the organism must be trained for its alienation at its very roots - the pleasure ego. It must learn to forget the claim for timeless and useless gratification, for the 'eternity of pleasure' "

- Marcuse, *Eros & Civilization*

This condition of compromise with the vision of ecstatic wholeness, total freedom, is the hell of spiritual death. Seldom in our part of the world does this lead to rapid physical death, by starvation; but it just as surely kills by industrial accident or disease, by weaknesses induced by long repetition, by road accident, by alcohol and drugs used in an attempt to 'de-stress', i.e. in an attempt to get into personal, ecstatic time, unmediated time. These things kill nearly everyone.

The cure for this exists only in small, temporary enclaves. The wizard is drawn ahead into liberation by the attractor at the End of Industrial Time, which actually consists of the *complete human being,* the virtual Superman who is perfectly liberated. This condition is of course impossible in the World; all freedom has to be measured by interaction with others, and others are still living in Dwarfworld.

There follows a model of how this notional complete human being descends through the Archons of industrial society, the Dwarfworld:-

0. Pure freedom; wholeness; the end of the Consumer Spectacle, the 'end of history'; the complete human being. The economics of this level are not even based on measured exchange: this is the world of the Gift.
*Inner Damage: none.*
This may become achievable on a large scale by new forces as yet unknown; in the present, though, the wizard can perhaps best glimpse it at the heart of a Temporary Autonomous Zone (see the writings of Hakim Bey).

1. Individual freedom; the highest that can be achieved in non-TAZ situations. At this level, the individual's Monstrous Soul struggles to retain its vision, to live rather than merely to exist. The wealthy self-employed person. This level also contains romantic images of crime seen as freedom, and freedom seen as crime; anarchist freebooters and privateers. An obvious question here is: How much freedom can money buy you? Some Libertarians claim to espouse this condition, yet they too confuse wealth creation with money making, confuse freedom with mere consumerism. As long as one is addicted to acquisition, the tendency is to slide down to level 3.

*Inner Damage: totality reduced to work, to the equations of survival - compromise is total, always. With good self-esteem, personal power is strong, so luck is good; individual can then work a minimal amount for his needs, and be free the rest of the time.*

2. Creative people under-earning. This level is where most magicians live.

*Inner Damage: self-esteem is poor; feeling of being second-rate; victim posture ingrained even in creative or magickal people. Tendency to accept full-time employment or inadequate state handouts.*

3. Wage slaves; the corporate ladder starts and tops out here. It makes no difference in terms of quality of life - i.e. real wealth - whether you are a shop-floor worker or a managing director at this level: it is all compromise in order to 'survive' even though the basic criteria of physical survival and relative comfort are more than satisfied.

*Inner Damage: total acceptance of formula of survival; all vision denied or actually lost; resentment of those freer than himself; death by work.*

3. Acute poverty, threat to actual survival.

*Inner Damage: as above, but with poorer self-esteem, so that individual feels all the stress of being in Dwarfworld, the survival formula, without even any material comforts and fun.*

# INFLUENCING THE MACRO-ECONOMY

The macro-economic system has some features which are decidedly vulnerable to magick. For instance, it seems that economists & econometrists cannot measure the money supply with usable accuracy. For instance, take the 3 parameters of output of goods & services, money spent on these goods & services, and people's wages and shareholders' profits. By definition, these 3 variables should be the same: what people spend (including what they spend on services such as savings) should equal the cost of goods and services bought, which in turn should equal their incomes. In practice, economic measures of these parameters often differ by 4 - 5%. With such seemingly simple measurements made so inaccurately (inaccuracy here is of the same order as growth, inflation etc), it is obvious that economics is not only not a predictive science, but doesn't even have ways of measuring its simplest parameters.

Another interesting parameter is called 'confidence'. This appears to mean trading expectations, as polled from various businesspeople and pundits. Stagnant economies can be re-inflated by a burst of 'confidence'. What we have here is a self-fulfilling prophecy, and anywhere we find self-fulfilling prophecies, we are in a magick-sensitive environment. The adventurous magickal businessperson might like to take this idea and, using the concept of 'confidence' as a magickal emotion, attempt to influence the macro system.

These features introduce genuinely chaotic elements into the system, and these are very simple examples; any magician who is knowledgeable about economics can find far richer and more complex sources of chaos in the global economy. And may wish to exploit them...

# APPENDICES

# APPENDIX 1:
# DISCOVERY WRITING

One of the techniques you will find extremely useful for the exercises in this book, and for numerous other situations where you need to think creatively, is known as discovery writing.

Discovery writing occupies a position on the language spectrum between conscious critical thought and unconscious automatic writing. It is a technique for expanding creative thought by the use of semi automatic writing in the form of rapidly scribbled lists. It is almost impossible to exaggerate he usefulness of this technique for breaking through the habit of self criticism that shrinks your creative thinking.

The whole idea of discovery writing is to do it quickly. Practice with a list of no practical importance, as follows:

1. Take a sheet of paper, and write at the top "20 USES FOR A TURNIP"

2. Write down the left hand side of the page the numbers 1 - 20.

3. Look at a clock or watch, and give yourself 2 minutes to complete this exercise.

4. Start writing, and don't stop. If you find yourself pausing, then write anything down; it doesn't matter how absurd or irrelevant. It doesn't even have to be remotely relevant to the title of the list: the point is to bypass the mental critic until the end of the exercise. Do it, do it fast, and don't stop writing!

Some further guidelines on discovery writing:

1. If you think you are going to have difficulty thinking up 10 ways of increasing your income (for example), then make your list even longer. Do 20 or even 30; as in some martial arts, the essence of this technique is to aim beyond the target.

2. Don't do it with the intention of picking the best ideas out as you write. This will engage the conscious critical faculty and vitiate the creative flow. There is plenty of time after you have completed the list to discard the nonsense and pick out the gems.

3. Let it be OK if you come up with a whole list of rubbish. You can always do it again - it only takes two minutes !

Now try it on a few lists that are important to your magick.

# APPENDIX 2 :

# THE PERCENTAGE BUDGET

A useful technique for analysing and planning personal spending is the Percentage Budget. This shows you what percentages of your income you are spending on all categories of your life. It is worked out as a percentage rather than as raw figures in order to leave room for income variation. It is particularly useful if you are self employed and therefore responsible for paying your own salary. It works as follows:

1. Keep a record of all your expenditures for at least one pay period (usually one month). Write own everything you spend in a pocket cashbook. Where you forget, estimate.

2. Break down your expenditures into fairly broad categories, such as Food & Household, Entertaining, Transport, Going Out, etc etc.

3. Calculate your monthly expenditure on items you are billed for. For instance, if you are billed every 3 months for electricity, take an average over a whole year, if you've still got the bills, or estimate it as best you can if you haven't. Add all such categories into your expenditures record.

4. Satisfy yourself that everything you spend money on is included in the system somewhere.

5. Now turn these categories into a percentage budget: Add together all expenditure, and calculate the percentage that each category represents. For example, if you spent £900 in the month, and £45 of this was on transport, your transport percentage budget was 45/900 = 5%. Do this for all the categories.

6. The Percentage Budget you have created shows you what percentage of your income you spend on anything. It can be used as follows:

a) If you wish to increase expenditure on any category, you have to take it from another category. For instance, you might at present be committing nothing at all to servicing debts. The debts simply get worse as they accumulate interest. Decide on a reasonable percentage to set aside for debt repayment, and decide which other categories will have to suffer to make this up.

b) when your income increases, you can plan how your new wealth is to be used to maximum effect.

c) you can decide what your priorities are, and how these are reflected in you patterns of expenditure.

d) you can plan saving and investment with much greater clarity.

# APPENDIX 3:

# WELL FORMED OUTCOMES: AN NLP TECHNIQUE FOR CLARIFYING INTENTIONS

Magicians can benefit from using some of the techniques of Neuro-Linguistic Programming (NLP). Effort is often wasted enchanting for inappropriate or sloppily-defined goals. One handy technique from NLP is called Well Formed Outcomes.

Goals are more likely to be achieved if they are:

1. Stated in the **positive**;

- i.e.: What do I want? (As opposed to 'What do I not want?')

2. Placed in appropriate **context**;

- When, where and with whom do I want this?

3. Expressed in **sensory specific** form;

- What will I see, hear and feel when I have achieved this outcome?

This way, you will know when you are achieving what you want.

4. Initiated and maintained by **self**;

- Is there anything in the world that is standing in the way of my getting my goal?

- Am I in charge of all the changes required? Magicians are often unrealistic on this point, and thereby waste time doing spells where there are too many wild variables outside the enchantment.

5. **Preserving the positive** aspects of the present state;

- Will I lose anything I have now by gaining this goal? And if so, do I value what I lose?

6. Of appropriate **size**;

- Is it big enough to motivate me? (Consider making it bigger)

- Is it small enough to not seem completely unrealistic? (Consider breaking it down into subsidiary outcomes)

- Is it worth the effort I shall need to put into it?

7. Having positive **consequences**;

- What are the consequences of achieving this goal (for me and any others I consider)?

- How will my life be different?

- Does it fit in with what I am and what I want to become? (This is a question about your values).

Overall, the technique helps develop one's sense of the congruence of a desire, how 'right' it feels.

These points are a good structure for clarifying goals, and they help keep you focussed through the process of achieving your goal.

# APPENDIX 4 :
# A MAGICKAL RETIREMENT

For those who wish to experiment with a highly structured and extremely persistent approach, I based the following extended series of workings on a period when I solved many of the problems I had previously encountered in wealth and money magicks. It is given in two versions, the second more intensive than the first.

It is called : **THE WHEEL OF CHAOS**

This is a Magickal Retirement of the Wheel or Disc, attributed to the magicks of money and wealth. It is a framework for the intensive study of Wealth Magick. Its objectives are:

1. To gain proficiency in Money and Wealth Magicks

2. To identify the sphere of material power and competence one desires, and make it happen.

The primary magickal weapon, as for all Retirements, is the Diary. Specific to this Retirement is the Chaodisc. The Pantacle symbolises the magician's world; the Chaodisc is the Pantacle of infinite freedom to construct your world.

It is made as a disc, slightly larger than the largest coin in your money, and about 4 - 5 mm thick. On one side is painted or engraved the Sigil Of Chaos. It serves as a magickal Pantacle for your rituals, and as a constant reminder of the nature of your Retirement.

## THE CATECHISM OF DISCS

*In the Aethyrs, Money is a Spirit, a pattern of information*
*In the common illusion, Money is the basis of Wealth*
*To me, Money is a parameter whose value is arbitrary*
*I am no poor slave of money; I, Sorcerer, wield the Powers of Chaos*
*I bind to me the Spirit of Money; I bind it by love.*
*I love Money, and Money loves me*

This Catechism may be altered or extended at will, as inspiration dictates.

## PHASE 1:

This Retirement should be performed for a minimum of seven days.

a) Carry the Chaodisc at all times, mixed up with one's coins.

b) Perform a Banishing Ritual, followed by the Catechism of Discs each day on rising and retiring. One purpose of the Catechism is as a daily reconsecration of the Chaodisc.

c) The Offering: after each morning performance of the Catechism, place a token sum of money on your Altar or place of working. This is added to with each morning Catechism. Choose a rate of ascent of your money offering, stretching what you imagine to be your means to their limit and beyond. For instance, £1 on the first day, £2 on the second, £3 on 3rd, etc. This money will be disposed of in what ever way you decide, based on your meditations in the course of the Retirement.

d) The magician will have devised at least one full Ritual, to be performed daily, on the theme of Money. Every form of money magick that you can imagine should be considered.

## PHASE 2

This Retirement should be performed for a minimum of 2 weeks. It involves a shift of emphasis towards Wealth.

a) Carry the Chaodisc at all times.

b) Perform the Catechism of Discs three times daily; on rising, in the afternoon and before retiring.

c) Each Catechism is followed by a spirit journey or meditation, to discover what material powers one desires. These observances may lead to subsidiary rituals to divine, evoke and illuminate your desires and their relationship to your present sphere of competence.

d) One major Ritual a day, to enchant for specific objectives revealed in the course of your observances. Areas that will be worth investigating include:

    1. *The Alphabet of Financial Desire*: Devise a system of sigils for each aspect of money and wealth. You could use Spare-style sigilization, bindrunes, or other suitable glyphs.

2. Work out enchantments to help each aspect that you want to work on.

3. Devise a way to tap into belief in connectedness with vast sources of money and wealth and resources. A positive version of the way chain letters operate, a level of psychology which generates 'money-egregores' which are fed by people's superstitious attention to their instructions - like wordviruses.

# APPENDIX 5:

# EVALUATION OF SOME TECHNIQUES

### 1. MONEY SORCERY: SIMPLE ENCHANTMENT

*EVALUATION:* Doing sigils or spells for money has a similar rate of success to most other forms of basic enchantment.

One of the differences is that most people desire or need more money more frequently. This means that many sorcerers favour the use of a servitor or other form of spirit suitable for repeated workings.

### 2. WORKING WITH THE MONEY SPIRIT
### *MONEY IN THE SPIRIT VISION*

*EVALUATION*: This approach is essentially the beginning of a sequence of workings; the Spirit, or your experience of it, will probably suggest what the next stage should be. If you can get good communication with the Money Spirit, this is a very promising approach.

## 3. GAMBLING

*EVALUATION:* Having dismissed gambling earlier, there are however two aspects of it which are of interest to the practicing magician.

Firstly, it is always a good idea to have some big payoff, low probability gambles on the go. Fill in your Pools coupon ( and don't forget to post it off!), buy your lottery tickets. Do it without lust of result, do it as a habit which barely impinges on your consciousness, and doesn't stop you getting more money in the meantime.

Secondly, it is sometimes worth experimenting with low odds gambling, such as fruit machines or races. Gambling machines, with their low stakes and payouts which won't change your life, can be used sparingly by the wise magician who wishes to investigate the symptoms of luck in his consciousness. If you feel lucky, give it a go, and see if your feeling was correct.

Betting on horses and dogs can be approached through divination techniques. Reports seem to indicate that the use of synchronistic occurrences is the best form of divination for racing. The names of horses and dogs are quite likely to turn up in the course of a day's 'random' intake of information, and so provide a guide to placing a bet.

Betting at Casino tables is generally a poor game for the magician. The best results are obtained with intelligently constructed systems. That some such systems work is attested by the fact that Casino staff are usually on the lookout for anyone who is working a system.

It is important to understand that, generally speaking, gambling is a form of entertainment for those so inclined, not a source of ready cash. An attitude of fun will improve your relationship with luck, and give you some protection against a sad addiction.

### 4. ZONE OF AVAILABILITY

*EVALUATION:* This exercise is particularly useful if you are interested in possessions, but not so bothered about money, for which it doesn't seem to work so well. However, the general approach of building upon the habit of becoming wealthier is valid at every level of wealth.

### 5. LUCKY HOODOO SPIRITS

*EVALUATION:* Another very ancient form of magickal work is that of making pacts with spirits or demons. The magician feeds the spirits, and the spirits obey the requests of the magician. Such pacts can vary from the elaborate and often bloody conjurations of the mediaeval grimoires, where a good deal of the gnosis is compounded of fear, and the stakes are usually high, to more 'informal' techniques in which the magician is not so alienated from the Spirits.

In Hoodoo, the magician forms a relationship first with the Hoodoo Spirits, invoking them and feeding them with attention, words, biofield energy and sexual energy, until the Spirits become familiar allies. From this base, the magician makes a contract with the Spirits: that he will invoke them and feed them regularly, repeating his prayers, until his desire has been obtained.

This might sound odd to many a modern magician, and to expound such a system thoroughly is way outside the scope of this book. Suffice it to say that, if a sympathetic contact is made with such Spirits, the results can often be excellent. My own early work in money magick was facilitated enormously by using such a system: the first few chapters of Michael Bertiaux's *Voudon Gnostic Workbook*. This is an off-the-peg system of evocation and invocation reprinted from the *Grade Papers* of the Monastery of the Seven Rays. There are three money/wealth workings in this system: a very basic, general spell; a gambling magick technique (which was not to my taste) and the *Contraite*. The latter is a
form of contract with the spirits in which the operator feeds them energy, and they do the money magick. I used this in the context of a prolonged working, which proved exceptionally effective.

Please review this book!

**The Author**
I'm a breathwork coach and chaos magician, and my writing is fired by my explorations of miraculous healing and breathtaking synchronicities. What is too big and weird to fit into my non-fiction books on magic and breathwork gets used to create the other realities I write about in my short stories and novels.

You will find a selection of my writings on my website at www.chaotopia.co.uk.

I was an early editor of the seminal journal Chaos International, and have been active for many years in the I.O.T. (Illuminates of Thanateros) and the Rune-Gild.
I teach at Arcanorium online college of magic, at www.arcanoriumcollege.com.

Visit the Facebook page http://www.facebook.com/KingdomOfWessex , for David R. Lee's fictional Kingdom of Wessex and other magical places. The Kingdom of Wessex is a setting in the novel The Road to Thule, and its origin will be revealed in the prequel novel The Cull, presently in preparation.

For occasional blog entries on all sorts of stuff, from cosmology through to paganism via chaos magic and the Northern mythos, follow my blog at http://chaotopia-dave.blogspot.com/.

My current projects include the prequel to my recent novel 'The Road to Thule'. In the non-fiction area, I'm working on 'The Breathwork Handbook', an in-depth study based on nearly 20 years of breathwork practice, and an examination of the magical and transpersonal dimensions of connected breathwork.

I'm happy to correspond about breathwork and related issues, email me at dleeahp@inbox.com.
I am based in Sheffield, UK, and spend quite a bit of time in London as well.

# OTHER BOOKS BY DAVID R. LEE

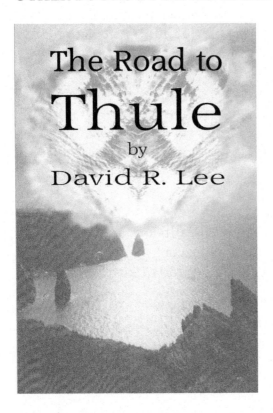

## The Road to Thule

'Souls such as ours bear within them the terrible energies of cosmic fire and ice, the anvils of the giants. We are of the Allfather's brood, and were forged for something greater, something that reality shatters on. You are of that bloodline, Alex, and you will come to know it.'

Exiled from his pleasant life in the heathen Kingdom of Wessex, Alex Tyler embarks on a journey through the flooded British Isles' archipelago of tiny nations, to the far North. There, he is swept up into the power of Thule, masters its secret magical technology and becomes the warlord who will save his people.

As Wessex and the other nations of the British Isles lurch into outright war with monotheist fanatics the Pure Light, the outcome will depend on two strange technologies. The problem is, one of them is deadly for any but a tiny, genetic elite to use, and the other, only Thule knows about.

## From Chapter 1: The Chilterns

Thania came half-awake to red light spilling over bare cement-block walls from the high slit of a window. In her dozing mind an image-track played, of a school-years video-feed from the day of the Burning City, the screen overloading with the brutal light of the nuclear flash. Then the scene jumped – she was in her lab at University, her skin frying in the heat of vonnie overload. She jerked awake, the dream-pain resolving into the shock of the raider-alarm shrilling under her skin, then she and the other three women were jumping out of bed, throwing on their land-and-water gear and scrambling for the amphibious craft.

They sprinted out of the low bunker across the cracked old asphalt, Thania twisting her strong shoulders through the unfamiliar straps of her pack. The night bloomed into rolling orange and black as the second fuel tank went up. The troops piled into the craft, which lurched out into a landscape of black mud lit by laceworks of fire.

Thania joined the backup team on the big land-and-water craft, their mobile base. It was a clear night ahead, away from the blaze. The two lightweight craft she'd learned to call Ducks sped north up the Thames Channel, picking up a radar trace of the retreating raider. As scout, her brother Duncan would be on the front Duck.

Thania looked round. Everyone was bent to some task. She turned to the stocky woman who'd just finished handing out ammunition. 'Freya, tell me what's going on.'

Corporal Ward looked up at Thania and smiled tightly, facial muscles flexing in the blaze of some stimulant. 'Pure Light Duck with six, maybe seven in it stripped a farm at Blewbury then took out the Wantage fuel depot.'

Thania nodded. 'What are we going to do?'

'At some point, they land, to hide from us. We catch up with them and use our last few rockets.'

'And then?'

Ward shrugged. 'We shoot at them.' She slapped at a mosquito on her neck and turned back to her work.

Thania stayed standing, wide awake now. Eighteen hours ago, she'd been undergoing her induction training and swallowing a gloopy sol of von Neumann seeds, fast ones that would grow under her skin into a transceiver of networked nanotubules. Three days before that, she'd received her MD from Bristol University and, against her brother's express advice, but thrilled and inspired by Duncan's tales of service as a scout, she'd joined up as a medic in the same unit as him, Prince Siward's Wessex Specials.

They'd given her very basic instruction in driving their main assault vehicle. 'This is called a Duck,' said the instructor, 'either in honour of its twentieth-century ancestor, the DUKW, of which this is basically a lighter, more efficient descendant, or through a lack of inspiration in the naming of military vehicles designed for a world of mud.' He turned and looked at each of them, the battered steel of his prosthetic hand gleaming as it flexed. 'You will learn to drive one. Wessex Specials are a multi-skilled elite.'

Half an hour later they cut their engines. A half-moon was rising, and Thania saw their two Ducks up ahead and a dark hump of land forming a horizon in the cold light. Something flashed up there, and the distant crack of a weapon sounded, some small projectile that never reached its target. Her keen eyes picked out something moving over the horizon line, and she felt a rush of gratitude in a soft, sudden ache in her knees.

The three craft headed for the muddy beach and crunched up the slope, the old engines screaming. It was moon-bright now, and as they moved cautiously up the hill Thania could see down to their left the remains of a town shattered by war, ghostly stumps of buildings on a lip of land above the black water. She supposed it was Princes Risborough, and swallowed nervously; her unit regarded the Chiltern archipelago to the north of there as Pure Light territory.

Pursuit was easy. The Duck they were following gouged up the soft turf, leaving massive muddy tracks on hard ground, and their infra-red picked out its heat-plume in the swathes of cloud-shadow. As they crossed the rise of the land and began their descent they could see the enemy craft clearly. It was obvious they were following a crippled vehicle. Ward passed Thania her binoculars and she saw it veering about from a damaged track-wheel. She swung the glasses round. Down there was Great Missenden, presumably where the raiders would have to hole up.

At the bottom of the hill, the two Ducks in the front started a cautious approach through the darkened main street of the little town. Everyone was aware this could be an ambush, and Thania had a strong urge to use the toilet.

Soon, it started to look as if they were just pursuing a lone craft down an empty road. Right in the centre of the town they saw the raiders' Duck parked across the entrance to a big old redbrick pub. They halted just as a volley of shots rang out from an upstairs window, gravel chips flying up from the road in front of them. Thania heard a grunted curse from the front vehicle, someone hit. Their crews turned the two Ducks side-on and dove behind them, returning fire with their assortment of weapons.

She saw Siward crouched behind the front vehicle with a rocket launcher, and then two of the rear crew dashed out, hugging the walls of the old buildings.

She recognized Sergeant Scott, whom she'd met only a few hours before, just as the defenders turned their fire on her and she spun, catching the momentum of the bullets in her body.

Then Thania saw Siward stand up, fire a rocket and dive back behind the vehicle. With shock, she watched the front of the big pub disappear in a flash of flame, and that was it, the battle was over.

It was getting light now. Thania let the absence of gunshots sink in for a full second, then jumped over the side of her vehicle and ran through the drifting smoke. Scott was dead, her eyes open to the sky. Thania turned aside briefly to vomit, before forcing herself over to the Ducks to check if everyone else was OK. She kept looking round for Duncan, and then she saw him swagger towards her, bright red neckscarf and curly red hair framing his grin, which struggled for supremacy with a frown of disapproval. Thania wanted to look professional, and refrained from hugging him, but let the wave of relief show on her face. His expression settled down to some kind of acceptance, seeming to say: *You may still be my little sister, but you're grown up now, and you're here.*

They looked over the ruins of the pub. There was no-one left alive in the rubble and they checked out the other large buildings along the street, selecting three for a base camp. Right next door a row of beautiful old cottages started, now ruined by war and the carelessness of troops. She hoped it wasn't Wessexers that had been so disrespectful as to shit on the floor.

Corporal Ward bustled round with a clipboard allocating quarters. Thania's care room was in the central building, another pub, but her one charge, Private Evans, was walking wounded, so he would berth as usual. She sat him down and dipped a nanoculture strip into the blood on his arm. 'Any fever?'

Evans shook his head. 'I feel fine.'

She gazed at his face while she dressed the wound. Like most of them, he was peppered with mosquito bites, any one of which might have infected him with vonnie seeds or other toxic nanites.

'What's your Raymond-Kowalski rating?'

'Ten.' He smiled, enveloped in the aura of her professionalism.

'Same as me.' She finished tying the bandage and checked the culture strip. A faint blue line showed above the pale orange of the blood, like a watermark. It barely touched '11' on the numbered paper. Evans had none of the high-level, more dangerous vonnies in his system, but he might just get a reaction. She reached into her bag and drew out two white capsules.

'Take these, to be on the safe side. Elutol, a vonnie-purge. Come straight back if you get any fever.'

Evans swallowed the pills. She smiled. 'OK, we're done.'

When she was alone, she checked her stock of nanoculture strips and elutol pills. That's good; enough to train everyone to use them themselves. If the unit got split up (or I got killed, she thought, frowning), at least no-one should go down with vonnie fever.

That was it, for now. Her responsibilities towards Maisie Scott had been discharged when she'd signed her death certificate half an hour before. She was arranging her equipment round the room when Corporal Drake came in. She smiled, admiring his masculine good looks, and he announced that the supplies team had found a fairly fresh rainwater tank on the roof, good enough for washing in, so she found the upstairs bathroom and took a lukewarm shower. She'd just dressed again when a beep under her skin told her it was coming up to six o'clock, so she joined the morning briefing in the main bar room.

Prince Siward, tall and sturdy in clean combat fatigues, blond hair pushed back over his broad shoulders, announced there would be reconnaissance missions straightaway, to check how secure their position was. Then they would honour Sergeant Scott and there would be two hours rest. They filed out, Thania catching Duncan's eye, and he winked at her as he crossed the cracked pavement to his motorbike. The scouts were so important to the expeditionary forces now there were no helicopters. The whole skill-base of air transport was nearly lost, it was so long since the fuel had existed to feed such monsters.

After the brief burial ceremony she went back into her empty care-room and gazed out of the window. The whole town was deserted. She'd had a moment of horror when Siward had fired on the pub like that – she was used to the swarming towns and squatter camps of her homeland, where every tiny terraced house, every hovel, counted as accommodation for at least one family. In Wessex, fire a rocket into any building the size of that pub, and you'd kill fifty people. Here, the terror of the long war surging back and forth through their streets had driven everyone out of the southern end of the Chiltern archipelago.

Being excused watch duty, Thania dozed in a chair in the care room, hypnotized by the patterns of the sunlight on the shiny, yellowed walls.

The shrilling under her skin woke her with a shock. These high-performance vonnies would take some getting used to. She shook out a numb foot and went over to the reconnaissance briefing in the main bar.

It didn't take long – scouts Duncan and Terry both reported an empty archipelago as far as Tring. No doubt Berkhamsted and Luton were still in Pure Light hands.

Siward stood up. 'We shall reconnoitre for one more day. If we find we've secured this part of the Chilterns for now, we go home.'

He turned slowly, gathering them all into his level gaze. 'That means we won't be on home soil in time for Harvest Festival. I say we have our very own Harvest party, here in Missenden, tonight.'

He dismissed them, and Thania found herself yawning in Freya Ward's face as they left the bar. Ward grinned. 'Tired?'

'And wanting to party,' said Thania. 'What was that you were on first thing, cocaf?'

'Vonnie settings,' said Ward.

Thania's eyes widened. 'Whoa, full metabolic control! So what's your R-K, 14?'

'I'm a 15. Want me to do an entrainment on you?'

'Sure – it'll be a first. My experimental subjects talked about entrainment, but none of them succeeded with me.'

They walked up the street in hazy sunlight and entered Thania's care room. Ward frowned thoughtfully at her. 'You've gone from doing vonnie tolerance research to joining the Army; what's the appeal?'

Thania sat down and was silent for a beat or two, choosing her words carefully.

'I believed in my research. Then it ended.'

'What were you working on?'

'High-end stuff. I was trying to find people who were tolerant beyond RK15, in the super-vonnie range. You know Raymond called them becters? He believed they could amplify quantum effects in the human Bose-Einstein field. I wanted – or dreamed of – something to give us hope again. Since the floods and the gigadeaths, since the loss of that glittering world, what do we have left? Vonnies is about it. I thought if I could isolate the features of nano-assembly that led to intolerance, we might be able to test Raymond's claims about those other powers that his becters were supposed to bestow on those who could tolerate them. But I hadn't found anyone with unambiguous becter tolerance by the time they...' she exhaled, her breath deflating her.

'You've tried high-end vonnies yourself?'

'On a regular Raymond-Kowalski, I'm only tolerant up to ten, so I wasn't a good subject. I'd inject myself with vonnie seeds in an ascending scale, a hypo of eluter to hand, but every time I got above ten, I'd go straight into fever. I'd leave it a day, then try again, hoping my immune system would get used enough to the vonnies to give them a chance to start growing nets. But it never did. It wasn't that that did it though.' She looked at Ward, unable to hide the bitter disappointment of the memory. 'Wessex's research base is cunked. They just withdrew our funding, as if there was any other hope than becters on the horizon. And if those Pure Light idiots take over, there'll be no more vonnie research, no more dreams. So I went to fight for what was left, using what I know. I'm going to be checking the vonnie profiles of any PL we capture.'

'Yeah, any that let themselves be captured,' muttered Ward.

Thania reached into her side pocket and drew out a gold coin, old but still glorious, the inverted T of the Thor's Hammer on one side and the profile of the young King Edwin on the other. 'Wessex is practically all that stands in their way. And what is Wessex? Wessex is a dream. One man's dream.'

Ward eyed the gold, gleaming in the weak sunlight. 'A man who everyone loved,' she said.

'My Uncle Ambrose gave me this. He scripted Edwin's coronation back in '93, when he handed these out. Minted from the gold he raided from the flooded Bank of England.'

She put the coin away and looked up, mixing a tired smile into her bleak expression. 'So, this entrainment. What does it involve?'

'It's simple.' Ward stood up. 'You sit up straight, but comfortable. I'll be doing it around your head.'

'Doing what?'

'All I know is my Bose-Einstein fields can influence yours, and the effect lasts for up to a few hours. Now shush and let me do it.'

Thania sat quiet, feeling nothing but the warmth of Ward's hands on her skull. 'There. That should keep you going for a bit.'

'Thanks.' Thania smiled and stood up, stretching her legs and arms. She had to admit she felt a bit livelier already. A thought crossed her mind and her smile broadened. 'You know, I've never tried flash-flesh, I was always in such a hurry to flush one batch out and get the seeds in for the next experiment.'

She looked towards the door then turned back, grinning, to Ward. 'Thank you, Freya. Tonight should be fun.'

Buy The Road to Thule paperback from:
http://www.amazon.co.uk/Road-Thule-David-R-Lee/dp/1478152176/ref=sr_1_1?s=books&ie=UTF8&qid=1342552976&sr=1-1

And as a Kindle ebook from:
http://www.amazon.com/dp/B008HHD4L0

## NONFICTION BOOKS BY DAVE LEE

## CONTENTS

    Foreword to the First Edition
    by Phil Hine
    Foreword to the Second Edition
    Introduction : Chaos Magic : The Story So Far
    Chapter 0: Magic and Ecstasy
    *Interlude: Fractals for Chaos Magicians I*
    Chapter 1: Wealth and Money
    *Interlude: A Psychonautic Banishing*
    Chapter 2: Conflict and Exorcism
    *Interlude: Fractals for Chaos Magicians II*
    Chapter 3: Magic and Sex
    *Interlude: The City and the Tunnels*
    Chapter 4: Magic and Physics
    *Interlude: Landscape Vision*
    Chapter 5: Body Alchemy and Healing
    *Interlude: Name That Deity*
    Chapter 6: Chaos Illumination

    *Interlude: AOFE/The Chrononauts*

Chapter 7:   Ecstasy and the Quest
*Interlude: The Octoplasm*
Chapter 8:   Pacts With Spirits
*Interlude: The Galafron Rite*
Chapter 9:   Chaotopia?
*Afterword: When all our ways are wrought for love of Her...*
*Appendix: A Chaos Magic Bibliography*
*Glossary of Chao-Speak*

## Chaotopia!

Once one is fairly competent at practical sorcery, there is little of importance that remains to be said or read about the subject; the magician at this point tends to emphasize inner development in his work. It seems to me that Chaos Magic itself has reached this point; the basic ideas needed for anyone to construct his or her own system of sorcery and to hone their skills are already covered by the available books. What has been lacking so far is a Chaos magical approach to the investigation of the ecstatic states that underlie magical gnosis. This book, rather than trying to provide yet another slightly different flavour of Chaos technique, takes as its starting point the relationship between ecstasy and magic; between Chaos Magic and Chaos Mysticism, if you like.


**Buy Chaotopia! as a paperback from:**
www.chaotopia.co.uk

**Bright From the Well** consists of five stories plus essays and a rune-poem. The stories revolve around themes from Norse myth - the marriage of Frey and Gerd, the story of how Gullveig-Heidh reveals her powers to the gods, a modern take on the social-origins myth Rig's Tale, Loki attending a pagan pub moot and the Ragnarok seen through the eyes of an ancient shaman.

The essays include examination of the Norse creation or origins story, of the magician in or against the world and a chaoist's magical experiences looked at from the standpoint of Northern magic.

Buy it as a paperback from: **www.chaotopia.co.uk**

The aim of this book is to provide the basic know how required to start making high quality magical incenses for ritual, celebration and meditation. Over 100 ingredients are discussed, and over 70 recipes are given. For those who wish to formulate their own recipes, comprehensive Tables of Correspondences are included.

The most comprehensive and complete book on the subject available anywhere.

*"Burn to me perfumes!"*
*'...the smoke seems to act as a vehicle for your invocations, mantras and devotions via the vibration of the bodymind's biofield, amplifying them tremendously to potentiate the intention of the ritual.*
*A candle- or fire- lit sanctuary in a temple or in a woodland clearing where the glowing clouds of smoke seem to vibrate with the spoken words, swirl with the movements of the participants, and above all reach the nose in wisps of ever-changing unearthly fragrance...*
*...this is the stuff of which effective ceremony and ritual are made '*

**Buy Magical Incenses from**:
www.chaotopia.co.uk/aromatics

# Connect Your Breath!
**24 page saddle-stitched A5 booklet with 60 minute audio CD.**

In order to master Connected Breathwork (such as Rebirthing or Holotropic Breathwork), you will need a coach. After a few hours of coached sessions, you should have enough experience to do a full session on your own. Coaches aim to equip the student with enough experience to be able to work alone indefinitely if desired. The aim of this book is to support the student of breathwork in between coached sessions. The accompanying CD can be used as a 'virtual coach' for solitary sessions.

**Buy from**: www.chaotopia.co.uk/cyb

Printed in Great Britain
by Amazon